it was never Eden

Poems by Jeanette Willert

Negative Capability
PRESS
MOBILE ALABAMA

it was never Eden

Book and cover design by Cristina Delgado-Howard.

Published by Negative Capability Press
150 Du Rhu Drive, #2202
Mobile, AL 36608
www.negativecapabilitypress.org

Praise for Jeanette Willert's
it was never Eden

"The poems in Jeanette Willert's *it was never Eden* are what Mary Oliver called 'poems of place.' They are, for the most part, grounded in the green mountain valleys and rushing streams of Willert's childhood West Virginia. Yet, like Oliver's own work, they contain truths that transcend time and place, that reach across the years and the mountains between poet and reader and give us a good solid shake, or a slap, or, sometimes, a fleeting kiss."

> —Dargan Ware, author of *The Legend of Colgan Toomey*.

"This collection displays a deep understanding of the human condition -- the complexity of emotions, the landmarks of a lifetime, the frail beauty of a moment. I find myself reading these poems over and over, each time discovering something I recognize as true and real and universal, something that makes the spirit ache in affirmation."

> —Jerri Hardesty, publisher, New Dawn Unlimited, Inc

"*it was never Eden* is full of memory, nostalgia, reflection and exploration of place, self and injustice. There is much enjoyment in the individual poems but the whole is so much larger than its parts. To read the book from start to finish uncovers a complicated story that led this reader to think more deeply about her own stories."

> —Ellen Goldsmith, author of *Such Distances* & *No Pine Tree in This Forest Is Perfect*.

"Whether writing about home and family, the death of a precious friend, the loss and tragedy of a love that dies or the joy of another love that endures, Jeanette's poetry is rich with emotion and defiant, persistent beauty. Rich with metaphors, there's magic in her words as she endeavors 'to know the world, its hardness and beauty, its dictates and will.'"

> —Rita Aiken Moritz, 2017 Alabama Poet of the Year and author of *So You Love a Prodigal* and *Precious Poems*.

"In America's current fast-changing social structure, we can easily overlook events of the recent past that were once fundamental. In carefully crafted poems of *it was never Eden*, Ms Willert writes about times of differently defined moral values, but those of which we can all identify. She's not proposing these as times she wants to change, but rather as reminders of the value they've contributed to the poems she has cleverly composed. Her words recall events with astonishing visualization and consequence, allowing readers to establish their own levels of condemnation, remorse, or approval. She writes too, with honesty, of the implications and anguish of broken love, assuming that any regret or blame can best be established by readers. The three sections of poems in the book strategically weave the poet's perceptions of the warp of Eden's perfection and the weft of reality to create a masterful fabric of significance you'll want to share."

—Mike Wahl, author of Living Adverbially

Nature's first green is gold,
Her hardest hue to hold.
Her early leaf's a flower;
But only so an hour.
Then leaf subsides to leaf.
So Eden sank to grief,
So dawn goes down to day.
Nothing gold can stay.

—Robert Frost, *Nothing Gold Can Stay*

Acknowledgments

Many thanks to the following publications that published these poems, sometimes in different forms or with different titles:

Appalachia, Amour, **Alabama State Poetry Society Morris Memorial Chapbook Award.** New Dawn Unlimited Publishers, Vol. 15, December 2017.

> *We thought it was Eden.*
> *Burying my father,*
> *Friday night pint*
> *Going up the mountain*
> *A life lesson at the Daniel Boone Hotel*
> *A black and white photograph of my grandfather*
> *The life lie*
> *Going home*

Alabama Writers Conclave Journal.
> *Silver Sneakers class.*

Birmingham Arts Journal.
> *Going up the mountain*

Birmingham Haiku Festival Award.
> *Haiku*

Buffalo Evening News Poetry Page.
> *Immigrant wife, 1923.*

Charles Frazier's Anthology of Appalachian Writing, 2017.
> *A life lesson at the Daniel Boone Hotel*
> *A black and white photograph of my grandfather*
> *Going home*

Crosswinds Poetry Journal, 2020.
> *An island of ghosts*

Crystal Wilkinson's Anthology of Appalachian Writing, 2020.
> *Beyond blood and bone*
> *Kanawha's call*

Libretto, 2020
> *Everyday America*
> *Silver Sneakers class*

U-Rights Magazine, 2020
  A morning after

Verse Virtual, 2020
  Pandemic: March 26,2020

WINK, 2020.
  little black dress.

A sincere "thank you" to my local writing group in Pell City, Alabama, who listen to my reading of poems every month and their unflagging support. A thank you also to ASPS, the Alabama State Poetry Society, which has taught me so well and offered me a literary home. Special thanks to Rita Moritz, Myra Barra, Dargan Ware, Randy Hale, Roger Carlisle and my husband, Richard Willert.

Table of Contents

1
Home & Belonging

2
Love, loss & lies

3

The larger circle

1

Home & Belonging

> *Perhaps home is not a place but simply an*
> *irrevocable condition.*
>
> —James Baldwin, *Giovanni's Room*

We thought it was Eden

In the town of my childhood
we felt invincible
as Saturday matinee heroes.
Myth wrestled and laughed
through us
alive
as Batman, Cisco, or Roy and Dale.

We ran wild,
charging briars of mountain paths,
balancing like aerialists
on mossy river booms,
channeling currents
careening to the falls.

No one noted Time,
sly trickster,
stealing in,
nor the universe snickering
as our sudden wings
latched to a quickened wind
buffeting each on our own way.

When I think of those gilded days
I sometimes wonder
how this cautious little owl
took nest in me.

Kincaid

There,
the mountains are deep,
smelling of wet copper.

There,
water engraves ragged ravines,
rumbling, splashing downstream
over ancient stone
to the rush of the Kanawha.

There,
unyielding bones of cliffs and canyons
shove at the sky,
shielding the vein of valley below
in a damp, mossy sigh
so old, so old.

There
is my troubled home.

Kanawha's call

Sometimes it's the certain smell that takes me back
  that damp, loamy leaf rot that exhales down the mountains
  toward the great, churning Kanawha.
  I know I've never left,
    in one sense,
    though a lifetime has passed in other places, other homes.

Family asks, "Are you ever comin' home?"
Though I plan not, I say, "May be."
The truth is I might.

Memories convene in the folds of my mind,
  the smell of cornbread sizzling in a skillet,
  coal dust grit underfoot nearly everywhere,
  loud foaming falls of the river,
  communal church dinners,
  the schooling, knowing every neighbor
  a sense of being bound,
    by our hovering mountains.

So many people,
so many days and years stacked away,
yet the valley abides with me...
  in the leaf fall and smoke of an Alabama autumn,
  sounds of a rushing river in Tennessee,
  in a gospel song springing forth from the turn of a dial,
    driving west into Mississippi,
  in the Pittsburgh waitress' drawl as she takes our order,
  in the still, filtered light of an old wooden church in Virginia,
  in the stark snow-lined fields of central Ohio,
  in the morning crow of a rooster across our lake,
  in the settling evening song of cicadas,
  late in the day from our own rich earth.

Immigrant wife, 1923

"Even as a small child, I understood that women had secrets,
and that some of these were only to be told to daughters."
—Alice Hoffman, *The Dovekeepers*

Stranded in the wild, damp mountains of Appalachia,
young wife and mother,
you must long for Ulster,
for home across the great sea.

Before the coal fire warms the kitchen,
in the chill early mornings,
do you miss the smell of burning peat?
Do you long to return to Ireland?

You fill your husband's dinner pail
with warm biscuits, meat and water,
before he descends into the open maw of the earth
to strip her veins.

Alone, you write in your book
of dreams laced with mystery:
the fairy people, tales
that trailed with you across the Atlantic.

Here in this faraway place, this deep hollow,
old myths murmur to you.
Other wives, mail-ordered from war-torn Europe,
gather with you to tell their stories.

But when your husband reappears,
blackened from the mine,
as the moon struggles to be born,
you never share with him your book of dreams.

Friday night pint

Friday night,
      Grandfather would bathe all over,
      not just the necessary parts
      or those covered with coal dust.

Then,
      with hands that no longer came clean,
      he would slip
      from a basement rafter
      a pint to steel himself.

Upstairs,
      Grandmother, chore-tired,
      Baptist to the bone,
      would whiff the whiskey
      and bridle.

Then,
      the tired marital dance would commence...
      her tears streaming in a slow waltz tempo;
      his anger, a quick cut time..

Supper,
      indifferent to their discord,
      we ate our food,
      planned the paths of our lives.

What did we know of enmity,
      of love laced with knives?

A black and white photograph of my grandfather

I remember it like fear,
that photograph,
fear that blends with a frightening childhood place—
> *a child opening the meat-house door,*
> *a sudden heaviness of air clutches*
> *a lingering smell,*
> *cured hocks of dead hogs.*

In the photograph,
a frayed black and white,
light flickered on
a ring of ghosts,
white-robed,
hooded.

I had come upon it
stuck in a stack of family albums.
You, Mother, pulled it away,
slipped it back in place.
"Go out now and play."

Over time, the picture disappeared
as did my grandfather,
felled by a heart attack
surprising as a sudden, murderous impulse.
Last night, an update on the local news,

the camera focused in on
Klansmen disguised in their pointed hoods
orbiting a burning cross.

Later, I dream,
a memory of the long-gone meat-house arises.
> *I enter, afraid but resolute.*
> *Smoke floats...curling about a hanging man*
> *dangling like bear bait from a darkened tree.*

Beyond blood and bone

On the spiral staircase of DNA,
where you and I are fixed,
Newton Dooley,
great grandfather,
son of Virginia,
conscript into Rebel duty...
could we talk, you and I,
of the Confederacy,
of statues being shoved from staid pedestals,
of slavery, white privilege, and rage?

Your ruined eye sewn shut,
your left leg shorn below the knee,
would you lean back, exhaling your smoke,
listening as I speak?
Would you find any bond with me,
anything beyond blood and bone?

I could ask you troubling questions:
Did you sacrifice your flesh
believing you were superior to the African?
After the battles, settling into
farming life with your new wife,
why did you name your children
Dixie, Jackson and Seddon?
Could you not let old ideas go?

If we were to talk,
would you stoop to atone,
sorry for losses, yours and those you imposed
as you yelped through the leafy Shenandoah?
Or, stubborn Irish, might you rub
your bad eye, suck deeply on your smoke
and slouch, determined, into your deep myth?

I wonder, but fear...
you would have your say,
fixing your good eye on me,
that pale green iris flecked with copper—
so like mine, but an eye angry, intent on hate.

Though you owned no slave,
you served. Did you,
(just as the boys drafted into Viet Nam)
battle at first for devotion to duty
but later solely for your fellows?

Your flag still ripples in defiance
of our founding documents, the common good.
It waves from poles advanced in fervid hands
with grievance of the Black man, the foreigner,
a legion of perceived oppressors. Your cause,
Newton Dooley, not forgotten nor forsworn.

Our bond is blood and bone,
nothing more;
for my country is not yours,
my desires do not demand dominion,
my prayers are not like yours.

Shadows of a sickle moon

In the 50's,
Americans liked Ike.
Doe-eyed Doris Day
retained her virginity;
Lucy and Desi
slept in separate beds;
Dean Martin sang of "Magic Moments"
and we believed.
   What could go wrong?
   We had Elvis and James Dean,
   DiMaggio and Monroe...

In those days,
loose girls were outcasts.
Irene, from up the hollow,
was that girl.
Late on a Saturday night
in the anemic moonlight .
the loose girl,
like Pandora,
opened up
on the cold concrete steps
zagging down the mountain
from our school.

Aroused, four young men lay with her,
taking turns.
Then spent, shriveled,
hovered over her
marking their territory
before loping off, laughing,
a sickle moon tracing their shadows.

Monday morning,
word leapt like a heedless locust
locker to locker,
class to class.

On the hillside,
delicate violets wilted
in the noonday sun.
Bobby sat with me,
tall, blonde, beautiful Bobby.

"Did you do it?"
Head hung low, he nodded.
I thought of that loose girl
who got more than she bargained for.
I rose and walked away.

He called my name—
        and then again...

A life lesson at the Daniel Boone Hotel
1957, Charleston, West Virginia

Midnight, the hotel coffee shop counter
we waited,
  unaware Negroes could not be served.
We waited
  for menus that never came
teenagers, Black and White,
our swing band taking a break.
I was fifteen.

In time,
a young waitress, her skin the color of strong coffee,
broke the news...
  nothing for us
  —not even water.

Genevieve and James hung their heads, ashamed;
I burned for them.
How could this be?
Born poor
in Appalachia,
poverty had protected me
from our great, continuing crime.

On that fine spring night,
moonlight riding silver ripples of the Great
Kanawha,
I closed the door on that grand old hotel, heavy-
hearted,
with eyes wiser
  but, oh, so much sadder.

Burying my father

I miss the wake at home,
  the kind we used to have.

I miss the women
  with warm, covered dishes and homemade desserts,
  carrying them forward like sacrifices.

I miss the hushed tones
  wrapping about heavy-scented flowers flanking the casket,
  punctuated by occasional filtered laughter
  from rooms beyond.

I miss friends and family together,
  celebrating life, remembering their dead,
  emotions peaking and valleying,
  unchoreographed.

Today, for my father, we gather in a squat building.
whose thin white entry columns
were intended to lend dignity to sterility,
the matter-of-fact business inside.

At least the weather is real.
 A hard-driving January snow
 whipped into southern Ohio overnight.
 It stings at the grave site,
 welcome as a penitent's scourge
 cleansing the desiccated reek of the funeral chapel.

Behind us, the Muskingum rushes cold toward the Ohio.
We shiver through The Lord's Prayer,
Mother huddled in an angora afghan.
Red roses blanketing the casket seem startled
at the snow's assault.
They remind me of blood spilt and left behind.

The rawness of the air is a balm.

Sideswiped

At a Starbuck's in western New York's ski country, a
young woman sits a few tables away with her father, steam
from their coffee drifting upward as she leans toward him, her
hair forward falling. A constriction wraps my throat, tight
as a garrote. She cannot know how life will be without him.
I envy her ignorance of the axis of the world tilting, funnily,
finally. Like a dime novel detective, I watch. Their closeness
strikes hard as an infidelity, their affection an ache. Tears blur.
I am again angry. I did not know how special it was just to
be together, when he and I slipped away from family to the
Rose City Café in Charleston. We would order a cheap meal
so, later, we could afford coffee and lemon meringue pie.

After my strangled eulogy, his body cabined in a
coffin close by, a friend comforted, "Did you not know—your
father was your hero? Time will heal you." Yet, in this coffee
shop, years later, the sting lingers —I scratch fresh fang holes
until they bleed.

Reunion

Now you are gone, my father,
I can admit I thought I was going for you, your childhood,
your cousins, your life before me. Year after year, I would
drive you down Interstate 77, out of Ohio, south toward
home. Past Charleston, we'd escape the public face of West
Virginia, heading into her troubled soul. Up old route 61,
hairpin curve at Deepwater, Loup Creek on our right; to the
left, stacked rock shelves of the Appalachians with painted
biblical exhortations which scared me as a child.

Prepare to meet thy God!

At Kincaid, we would park at the new brick school, the
old wooden one gone when the mine closed down, gone
like the company store, the rented company house, the
Baptist church beyond the railroad tracks; gone like your
cousins and sister during the war to factories in Detroit
and Baltimore. You'd fling open the door and begin calling
to cousins, to friends, to your past. Your happiness was
contagious as Spring blossoming.

This year, up on the mountain, I wade through weeds to
family graves, some years tended, other years overgrown,
their simple presence precious, nonetheless. I sit in the wet
grass near them, sounds of our living family drifting up from
below. There is a peace in all this, a reunion born of blood
and time and place. Our mountains encircle our living and
our dead, their crests lapping outward, one behind the other,
far into the county. I lie back and breathe natal air, aware I
came here not just for you.

Mother, now ninety

Picturing her young, it's the shoulders
    that first give heed…
    muscled, brown, so strong she could swim the wild river,
    over and back
    laughing.

Today, she struggles to shed the sweater that seldom
    leaves her shoulders.
    The nurse makes herself scarce,
    squeamish of old flesh,

I lift a thin arm, tugging gently,
    the arthritic grip of the bones testing
    my will.

Disrobed, she waits, hunched
    on the examining table
    biding time, waiting
    for those who squeeze, prod,
    probe the shriveled shell —

Those ignorant of
  strong brown shoulders,
    a woman shoving rivers aside
    and returning laughing
    to the far shore.

The life lie

"If you take the life lie from an average man,
you take away his happiness as well."
—Henrik Ibsen, *The Wild Duck*

Quilting points, Ibsen called them,
effects that sustain our myths, our lies.
For my aging aunt,
hunkering in her decaying bunker,
all she owned mattered,
each piece vital as a Seurat dot,
a broken clock, hands frozen
at twenty to three;
a tall, broad bass, commandeering
the cramped hall landing
(never moved in my lifetime),
"You know, Bill played that
after he came back from the Olympics."
That happened about 1933.
Memories stuffed in attic boxes
not to be disturbed though
Death hovers the threshold.
Life and Look stacked on
dank basement shelves,
pages molded together.

Her letter of recrimination burns my hand
—formal notice
voicing a violation of her privacy,
my junking of old potting soil
and cracked flower pots.

Attic and basement, poisonous marshes
where the mythical girl still thrives,
love letters simmer,
pressed flowers bloom fresh, fragrant,
rising and falling
on a tremulous, expectant bosom.

We deal our cards;
the hourglass sand sifts slowly...her play.
She protests,
"You know, it will all be thrown out on the curb."
Exasperated, half-ashamed, I demur...
for I, too, am encumbered
by a life-lie.

Going up the mountain
after Billy Collins' *Directions*

When you decide to go,
head out the back path that quickly narrows,
if it is still there, before it gets lost
in that tangle of wild berries, pine saplings and old oaks.
Remember the way?
Beyond our failing fence
be careful of the outcroppings,
remains of the glaciers when they came gliding through.
I fell there once, scared
by a narrow slither of topaz and black.

Further along, you'll happen on what's left:
Creedy's old cabin, some brickwork of the chimney.
You'll be starting up the mountain
 bring a pole for the climb.
Soon, you'll hear the trickle
the stream should still be running
though fall is pressing upon us.
Follow it awhile. From there
you'll have to guess your way.
 I've never gone that far.

Who knows what you'll find.
Harry, in the old days, would hike that way to mind the antenna.
You may see what's left of it,
if you get that far. But he always carried a hoe,
rattlers love those dark cliffs.
You might be tempted to rest there in the shade;
but take care
you're not on the losing side.

When you decide to set out,
I will walk with you
a little ways, maybe gather some late berries.
You'll have to forge on by yourself, though—
I'm too old too attached to life
to tempt the wild.

On reading Jeannette Wall's
The Glass Castle

Perhaps our shared name hauled me headfirst
into the memoir. Perhaps Appalachia
has its tines so stuck in me I cannot resist
time surfing to my childhood,
those difficult people, the alcohol,
the instability, unconditional love
and big gardens that grew everything:
tall stalks of rhubarb and corn,
fragrant roses and fat, pearly gooseberries.

Perhaps, I understand too well the claim
the mountains establish early in your life
and will not relinquish. None of us born
there can tearlessly hear Country Roads
though we know there is hokum interlaced
with belongingness. Like the narrator,
I longed to escape. New York seemed possible,
but for me it was Chicago, then New York.

Perhaps, some would not understand her
turning back to her family, acknowledging her roots,
a decision prompted not so much by forgiveness
as by realization. You do go home again
because
you never left.

Home
 exhales a coppery breath
and wraps its weathered body
tightly around your D
                    N
                      A

Going Home

I would love to have lived out my years
back home again, in the damp mountains.
Even in decline,
the old Appalachians hold fast
to those of us born there.

But if I should return
all will be changed...
my people long gone
my own life nearing its end,
the farm grown over,
the house falling in on itself.
So much work
just to get going.

I don't want to farm.
Maybe some strawberries and pear trees,
try to revive the grape vines.
But no chickens, no hog,
no curing house, no long rows of corn,
I would be close to our beginnings—
the Hamiltons, Kincaids, Cales and Dooleys.
I could cut roses for them on Memorial Day,
clip the vines claiming their graves
and recall their days.

I could plant another great willow
just where the old one fell.
I could sit on the porch,
watch Loup Creek winding by,
hear the settling night sounds
as the moon peers over the ridge.
The gold glimmer of lamplight
at last beckons me inside.

To the boat house, again
after Elizabeth Bishop's *At the Fishhouses*

It is late November;
beyond the old boat house
a man sits fishing near an overturned rowboat.
His cast splashes, ring circling ring,
as the live bait sinks.
Above the outlined hills, sunset
has abandoned a pale, iridescent halo.

The river drums over the dam.
Pine and damp leaf exhale rot from the hills.
The boat house is open on all sides,
concrete pillars supporting the thin tin roof.
To get there, a narrow dirt path cuts away
from the Inn's manicured grounds.
Heavy gray pervades the scene, the surface
of the river as it pulses to the falls, mountain
shadows shouldering over the valley, up river
the New and the Gauley fork into the Kanawha.
Nearby, the pier and boom cut straight
charcoal lines into the river flow.
On the bank, weeping willows have thrown leafless
strands into the river's drag.

The fisherman unfolds another short stool.
He had been a childhood friend.
We talk about the disappearance of our school,
the new church built too close to the road,
crazy white-water rafters on the New River,
the decaying of our town.
He wears a high school *Traveler* jacket,
its red horse head crest faded to brown.

At the edge of the river, where boats from upstream dock,
tarred mooring posts are spiked every ten or fifteen feet.
Muddy, cold and deliberate,

bearer of bodies caught in merciless currents,
hawks and river rats do okay.
Once, a pair of bald eagles thrown off-course by a storm
Took a rest atop the rusting lifeguard rigging of the pier..
From a bench, I watched them
swiveling their white heads, feeling we were akin.

If I had remembered the words of *The Eagle*, I might
have recited Tennyson's poem. I only spoke the beginning,
"He clasps the crag with crooked hands,
Close to the sun in lonely lands..."
They pivot their feathered heads in unison at the strange human sound.
Then, as though in communion, turned to each other and rose,
their shadows streaking across the dark water
as they bore themselves homeward.

Muddy, cold and deliberate,
the river flows . . . on, and on.
Behind us, the town,
its twin row of company houses dwindle
to a single line where mountains begin closing in.
The old dwellings seem solid,
though to me they house ghosts,
tenants long gone.

The river goes on, as it has all my life,
as it flowed centuries before me,
as it will for millennia following millennia.
The water is cold, numbing cold;
it bestows a kind of baptism, elemental, eternal...
an opportunity, of sorts, to know the world,
its hardness and beauty, its dictates and will.

Caterpillar wings

Wait,
tucked deep within
an inching, fleshy fist,
earthbound,
longing
to uncurl
&
stiffen,

wait,

nascent,
ancient geometry
tattooing
onto trussed sails.

wait,

the deep, sacred shove,
marking their time
to flame forth,
to tremble
into agoraphobic air.

Set free!

Do they ever yearn
for the enveloping comfort
of their beginning?

2
Love, loss & lies

I want

To do with you what spring does with the cherry trees.
— Pablo Neruda, *Twenty Love Poems and a Song of* Despair

Listening to Elvis in a parked Chevrolet

When he told me he loved me,
    I should have turned the radio from Elvis' crooning
        to the sobering evening news;
            I should have thought of Ann Arbor, finishing my degree,
                I should have wondered how he would be at sixty-three,
            I should have…

When he swore he adored me,
    I should have pictured the quick temper flare;
        I should have considered his appetite
            for Camels and double Dewars,
        I should have…

When he kissed my trembling shoulder,
    I should have straightened my straps,
        buttoned my blouse,
            and run for home
                like Mantle rounding third.

        I should have…

Not All Loves Die the Same

Unlike Romeo and Juliet,
you and I limped on for years
in tepid bedrooms, gone flaccid with routine.
Tongues that once flamed
sharp as a slug of Southern Comfort
fail to stir.

Those women
in Chicago or LA
late evening, mid-week,
perched at the bar
sipping a cosmo,
arms bared in the lamplight...
why did you need them?
For the return of the sting?

Tonight in our bed
the sheets are cold,
your embrace
a language I no longer know.
Your kiss, dry as dust.

A morning after

A sense of spent frenzy
rises from a shambles
of shoes, shirts,
pants and underwear
cast aside in haste..

A blanket, nearly wholly off the bed
fails to cover the pair lying
back to back, breathing regularly
as morning musters into their lives.
On a night stand, a hotel map and menu,
torn condom wrapper and room key.

Morning light pierces a slit
where the curtains fail to meet.
A bitter smell of stale Scotch
eddies above cigarette stubs,
a few circled with a scarlet stain.

Phone b-b-r-r-r rings three times, wake-up call.
Time for work, conference meeting at nine.
A slow stretch as the man glances at
last night's prize who still looks
pretty good in the limp light.

A little later, she will be across the table
from him when business gets underway.
But for now,
a shower, and

—oh yes,
a call to his wife.

Thinking of Patsy Cline

Those near-**crazy** days,
I would drive aimlessly,
for hours, out of Nashville
into the rolling farmland
redolent of fresh manure
and spring mown hay.

Weighing our wilting and falling away,
I considered our days together,
days become dead and gray,
sparked at times by white-hot anger
so long held at bay.

I would drive slowly,
windows down,
the air still cold;
it slapped my senses,
an eager flagellation,
a scold.
I wanted to hurt.

Some days I parked near a deserted cabin,
a defeated wreck, **falling to pieces.**
A scramble of vines embraced it,
a wilding,
an attempt to defy neglect and gravity.

In the ruined yard
a remnant of a once **sweet dream,**
a congregation of yellow and white lipped
daffodils
bowed to the sun,
a ground report for the world
no longer seen.

Leaving Tennessee
after Robert Bly

As I drive north into Pennsylvania,
snow appears
in smatterings,
a demi-world,
in shades of grey and white.
The windows, steamed,
begin to trickle

Good-bye,
all my young life…

New York, hours ahead,
a future uncertain.

Awakening

This morning the rain roused me.
A heron's fractured cry
thrummed across the lake, drowning
small splashing sounds of spawning
near the shore.

A gray lizard slid across the window screen,
eyeing
a beetle cocooned in a glistening web near
the eave.
A flick of its narrow tongue sent the trap
aquiver,
dewdrops tumbling,
a silver flurry of fallen stars.

I think of your leaving,
the scoring of sharp words,
harsh as sandpaper
scraping
my flesh.

Temptation licks my ear

Ah, Snake,
why is it
you tempt us
with dark acts
that summon
the primitive self?

We succumb
to a fierce drag of salty undertow
embrace your siren song

—later
      surfacing,
         gulping,
            cursing,
the civilized self recovers,
murmurs the rescued's thankful mantra.

In a dark corner, the primal self
      licks its wet fur,
      curls and settles,
      pillowed into your coiled, cool nest.

Forbidden fruit—
Oh, how I want to taste you!

            why
                not?

What I said and what I thought...

Remember
the first time you spoke to me?

I do.

At Ruby Red's, Friday evening, happy hour,
the school day ended,
our teen-aged students freed for the weekend...

Scotch on the rocks in hand,
you sauntered from your chums
to me

and said:
    "I'd like to get to know you—
    in the biblical sense."

Took a moment to register.
I smiled and replied:
    "You need to get past the begetting
    and into the Beatitudes!"

But my mind said,
"Oh, he is so fine!"

Then we became lovers

Kismet,
serendipity,
fate or fluke,
Providence,
coincidence,
humdrum circumstance?

You
happened to be there.
I
happened by.

little black dress

When I was young and slender,
I had a black dress
cut low at the breast and tight at the hips.
Peau de soie. It whispered as I moved.

When I was young and slender,
I had a black dress
I wore with high, high heels
that tapped to a beat like the blues.

When I was young and slender,
I had a black dress
that swiveled heads like sunflowers as I passed
in days when desire flowed like lava.

I had a black dress
when I was young and slender.
It shivered to the mindless floor
when I met you.

Notre chanson

Love, will you dance with me once more,
whispering our song as we sway?
With that same song you call me back
so easily to your embrace.

Whispering our song as we sway,
tonight, I think only of you
of dancing in the summer night,
my dearest, as we used to do.

With that same song you call me back
the siren song I can't forego
the one you sang so long ago
the one I love as blood and bread.

So easily, to your embrace
I slip once more to you, to you,
my secret love, forbidden joy,
my serpent, my Eden, my all.

The way we are

You
are a sudden stab of twilight,
a star-sent spear to stop my heart,

You
are the raucous warning,
the tick of the clock that keeps me sane.

You
are not a cool jazz riff,
a smooth Cabernet, a metro-male.

I
am, perhaps, the beach mouse
who furbishes her dune nest
with small shiny treasures.

You,
though, will ever be
the twilight that spears my heart.

As day wanes,
I will hunker in my burrow
and wait for you.

At times...

At times, when tired or angry or old,
we relent,
acknowledge life as a death march.
Mostly, though, we ignore the inevitable,
diverted by hawkers and fairs,
rituals of the roadside.
Days pass in clown-face:
       side shows, peep shows, magic shows,
       ceremonies, contests of weight and wit,
       Sno-cones, paper wrappers of pastel cotton candy,
       cocaine, Coors, and on-line come-ons...

On the road, humping our loads,
we plod on,

the certain destination dead ahead,
exact location unknown as a buried IED.
Singly, we arrive,
but sometimes
an entire company falls at once.
With death, those on the approach pause,
mouthing to the living kin,
"So sorry for your loss"
 (as though an alternative exists).

Dance with me

"Only connect...and human love will be seen at its height."
—E.M. Forster, Howard's End

Do you dance my dance,
or do you move
to liquid beats
I do not hear?

But come,

let us dance together
our steps so different
let us dance through our days
and love each other anyway.

An island of ghosts

You didn't notice, did you?
That mob of years bunching, branching—
its weight strains the trellis of time.

Heavy leaves of living shaded your vision
as you wove your way through school days,
work days, family days,
holidays, pay days,
snow days,
Maydays...
Mayday!

You knew your place
by the feel of the thing.
You belly-flopped, floated, fishtailed,
the years bearing you
to this isolated island of age
where you and time embrace,
an estranged tango,
shifting suddenly on quarter notes
from myth-ed past
to a shaky, unchoreographed present.

Here, on this island of age,
ghosts are more real than the real.
Here, ghosts outrank any current online Amazon commodity.
Here, ghosts comfort as the woke world will not.
Here, ghosts guarantee there is a way out.

3

The larger circle

We clasp the hands of those who go before us, and the hands of those who come after us; we enter the little circle of each other's arms, and the larger circle of lovers whose hands are joined in a dance, and the larger circle of all creatures, passing in and out of life, who move also in a dance, to a music so subtle and vast that no ear hears it except in fragments.

—Wendell Berry

"Bite the apple"

a voice demands,
apple red as a laid open heart
hanging by so thin a thread.
Where are its fellows?
It glows alone.

"Bite the apple";
the voice beckons.
She considers, trembles,
no turning back.
Hands outstretch.

"Bite the apple";
the voice croons,
a soft welcoming.
Fingers pluck.
Treasure in her hungry palm.

"Bite the apple";
the voice invites.
("Seize the day!").
Myth, at this point,
records an error.

Eve swallows, savors, smiles.
        Now,
            she can know.
Which begs the question:
that voice...friend or foe?

The morning after death

The sweeping up the heart,
And putting love away
We shall not want to use again
Until eternity.
                    —Emily Dickinson

You wonder, don't you, why the sun rises
yet again, when your world is upside-down?
Yes, there was a "bustle In the house" this morning,
and death did come calling some hours before.

But, as to the "bustle", vital to
placing us, the living, back into the natural
flow. Natural as in… nature, human nature,
the nature of life from birth to death:
nature as in day and night, the turn
of seasons, the certainty of stars.

We "bustle" not in denial, but affirmation,
not in disrespect but affiliation.
We, too, will be dead, but in the future…
but certainly dead as our forebears,
their stories now dead with them.

The earth goes on, morning bursts
beyond the stand of pines across the lake,
and evening descends like a filmy drape
over those same pliant pines.

Last night, a full moon cast light
across the lake, like a lady
laying a long white glove
atop a glass table.

I think of you;
I think of tomorrow.
I think of when no one
will remember us
and that must be okay.

Educating Venus,
after Sandro Botticelli's *The Birth of Venus*

Watch her emerge,
winged wind gods blowing her ashore.
She ignores a figure offering a fine embroidered robe.

Witness her, fresh, stepping out
from the filigreed frame,
her red goddess hair trailing the wind,
no longer balancing aplomb the awkward shell,

Naked and assured,
she stands
an ecstatic sweep and flow of beauty.
She advances into wreathed shadows of laurel,
whispered weaving of bulrushes,
then turns in farewell
to the womb of waves washing ashore.

She is yet to endure
   rapacious attacks of the Dark Ages,
   tortures of the Inquisition,
   the chastity chains of Puritan theology,
   and manhandling of patriarchal law.
She survives those assaults
and others closer to home.

Today, she returns to begin anew.
She allows a light blouse to loosen
then shiver from her shoulders.
Her hand does not rise to cover an exposed breast.
She stands on centuries of shattered shell.
Behind her, a multitude now cries,
"Me, too!".

"Complement" without the "I"

It was a stunning sermon…
  "The Necessity of Complements,"
women as complements,
Complement with an "e",
  not an "I".

> *complement* as trimming
> *complement* as side dish
> *complement* as completing another,
>   not oneself.

That sobering sermon,
proffered rightful power to the testicled.
And the women of the parish?
Heads lowered, praying,
they knew they were lower-case.

> as a *complement*,
> I could not breathe.
> Words from that pulpit
> scatter-shot my sex.
>
> I rose.
> In my wake,
> carapace fragments
> fell to the aisle.
> A narrow canal
> opened to new spaces.

Things fall apart

And what rough beast, its hour come round at last,
slouches towards Bethlehem to be born?

Wm. Butler Yeats

Warsaw, 1939-

You part the curtain, Fraulein, curious, careful, a
primal urge to see what you have heard. A sudden scramble
of boots clatters on cold pavement. An abrupt thud, a crack
of wood thrown on wood, then the hammering of a coffin,
raw pine. Inside, a body, not a soldier, not a partisan, but
not a nobody: a son, a brother, a father, a gypsy or a Jew
tumbled helter-skelter into that rough box. Next year, could
be a ditch, an oven, a gas-fumed shower. Does it matter,
the destination? The body will not recall. Only the living
register, weigh what is foul, what is hideous, what cannot be
forgiven.

Decades later, we are caught again in the clamor of
honking hatred. Do we hunker before a screen to gape at
a vanguard of vandals? Do we recoil, as from the bruising
slam of a heavy weapon? Are we attuned, alarmed, as vulgar
voices weave like a lariat about us? Dare we confirm echoes
of 1939 - the hated bodies, smeared with yellow, marked as
"offal", a stench to destroy?

Idyll in Aleppo

I am watching 60 Minutes, a feature story on the bombings in Syria. Sweeping past crumbled apartment buildings, the camera slides inside one, focusing on a man in a ruined room. He inhales the drifting smell of nearby fires. Alone with his gramophone, he is playing Bach.

A wisp of smoke spirals from his pipe, streaming like a genie. I wonder why he is sitting alone there amid gray rubble that was once his city. He leans forward into the harmonic cascade of chords, one leg crossed over the other, listening, absorbed not by ruin but by defiant, persistent beauty.

Lament for Barbara Stevens

A late May day,
 a worn-down diner on Hertel Avenue,
we are lingering,
a few minutes to catch up-
the feature article you were sending out,
your heading to a Maine retreat-
then hurried hugs,
unfurling of umbrellas,
scuttling to our cars.

That Monday morning, we awake,
you, to the smell of pine, lure of a Maine lake
I, to a steady Buffalo rain.

That Monday morning we rise.
You splash into the cold of the lake,
          silver ripples sliding through your wake
I listen to NPR, curl my stubborn hair,
          needing a cup of Starbuck's Special Blend.

That Monday morning we go our separate ways.
You head for the distant raft and the open
          arms of God,
I gulp my coffee, dodging traffic on the 219,
          heading for the rain-shrouded city.

In strands of mist,
          you hoist your cold, wet body onto a lilting raft,
          lift your arms in joy,
          whooping your success.
          Early light caresses a halo about you.

Then, quick as a moving shadow, you collapse,
          your spirit slips
          away over the lapping waves,
          into the quiet cedars,
          their ancient, familiar scent
                    welcoming you.

In my first class I read Whitman:
   the star, the last lilacs,
   the loss of a great one,
   not knowing
      you are gone.

Boundless silence

Last April,
Charlie gave "Cancer Sucks" t-shirts,
to us for ferrying him
to daily chemo treatments.
We celebrated his remission
with margaritas on the deck.

Deep December,
snow in the air,
I tuck the Charles Thomas funeral card
with his smiling image into my purse,
reminded of his George Clooney charm.

> I recall a glacier in Alaska "calving",
> aqua shards, large as barges,
> falling from the core,
> slicing down like a guillotine,
> roaring into the icy bay below.
>
> I remember the glacier
> not so much for the hubbub of its fall,
> but for afterwards –
> the boundless silence.

Driving home,
I think of his wife,
how bereft she will be
once the house is emptied of family.

Beside the highway, I pass
the snow-covered corpse of a deer.
His legs poke upward,
as though braking
against the taking of his life.

Everyday America

Our Waffle House looks like all the others:
tired formica tables studded
with condiments and napkin holders,
a long line of fixed, metal counter stools,
faded leatherette booths tacky to the touch.

Today, outside the big plate glass windows,
business is brisk at the Shell station,
traffic on 231 seems to be moving along.
Behind the counter, a cook is shoving
hash-browns, onions and bacon over the wide, hot grill.

Overhead, the light cast by large, round globes
creates a bright operating room.
Five "girls" are handling the booths and counter.
I know them all.
I sit at one of Amber's booths.
She knows she is my favorite.

Her fingernail polish changes color when wet
I have learned over time, but I do not
know the stories of her piercings
or the web tattoo behind her left ear.
She looks tired.

She pours hot coffee and steps back a pace.
"My son died last week", she barely breathes.
"An accident?" I ask.
Her face is damp and doughy.
"He was twenty... overdose. Not heroin,
Fentanyl ." That fact seemed important to her.
He'd been clean for five months."
She sighs, her eyes teary, confused.

Behind her, the work elbows on.
Orders are called out, eggs, bacon and biscuits
slide onto plates, the jukebox pumps out country woe.
I rub her forearm, not knowing what else to do.
My limp "I'm sorry." is worthless,
so small, so impotent. It vaporizes with my breath.

Even here in our small Alabama town
a Hydra is preying,
its gargantuan multi-national mouths
stuffed with drug money sacrificed
every night by everyday America.

Dylann, the boy who became a killer

Somewhere in the huge mural of our world
that boy with lost eyes
bowl haircut
and clinking chain hanging from his jeans
could have had a place.

In a busy scene crowded with communal detail
had he been consigned to the bottom edge,
the lonely bank of a winding creek?
We might picture him there
pitching pointed rocks at passing fish
preparing for an angry burst that would
wholly alter the motion, coloring,
even perspective of that huge mural.

That boy.

Might he have been saved
had one summoned him
for chores or an idle game,
clothed him with care,
trimmed his hard edges
so that he fit, snugly,
securing a proper place
in that huge mural?

Not that boy.

In our time,
a warm June night in Charleston,
that boy with the clinking chain,
        reportedly high on Suboxone,
dead-eyed,
        with words of on-line hate sites seething,
took aim,
        —"88!"   "Hitler for sainthood!",
loading and reloading,
his hatred compressed
into slick, jacketed bullets
crashing from his .45.

Pulse

Orlando, June 12, 2016

On the screen,
a photograph appears, fades,
another takes its place.
One after another,
the victims appear so alive,
smiling, assured, flirting with the camera
as millennials do.
To the side their names and ages,
temporary markers before the grave.

Their bodies are strewn, bloodied,
amid the tumult, hot bullet casings.
A sulfurous smell of slaughter
drifts over them
as their cell phones peal,
pleading for response.

Grief has breached the public dam.
Tears choke the living,
the families, the survivors,
the responders, the country, me.
Death has crashed in far too soon.

Closing out

The last day has come—
good-byes and final reports.
A sigh of resignation,
all is done.
Successes validated, debts paid.
But failures like set stains refuse to fade.

That last day has dropped,
ready or not.
The hour is late, yet
you remain, missing those gone.
How had they cleared the way,
defying the hurry of those circling hands?

The last day sighs, impatient.
Turning loose seems hostile,
shove back, though, you must.
Rise now and go
to your rest.
Time will cover for you.

Cyber Prison

A morning email message urges, *"Update your account!"*
I begin this new day, cradling my steaming tea,
savoring its heat on a dark December morning.
"Your password is required"
a message now assails.

Set down the tea, go find the password cheat sheet,
the key to many kingdoms. Ah, glorious Zen!
The list found, a return to the request, only to read
"Update your password".
Movements, strict as a minuet, commence,

Sipping tea, cooler now, I type a code—
a pink streak flushes in with a warning,
"a capital letter and a number must be included."
I tap in a new code, noticing a chill to the morning.

A second swipes by, another pink alert,
"a minimum of 8 figures is needed".
Scanning my list for a password mate,
"Keep the herd small", I reason, as I pound anew.
"So, now what have I missed"?

"Password accepted!"
the *they* hidden in "the cloud" cheer.
My tea now tepid, I am not so chipper.
Return to the email and then check the cyber site
to ensure data is confirmed, secure as a zipper.

Site appears in bright colors, a musical interlude.
Password requested. I rap in the characters,
suspicious now of cyber subterfuge.
"Incorrect password".
"Damn!"
and the tea is cold.

Silver Sneakers Class

Begins with Buddy Holly.
The women rise and march,
 step side to side.
The men short now on testosterone,
 sit, shuffle their feet and do bicep curls.
Mr. Combs abandons his cane
at the door and drops himself into our care
as in one of those group trust exercises.
We provide.

Buddy Holly, forever young,
belts out *That'll be the Day*, and we
who once jitterbugged the shine off the linoleum
sway and march, scoop and lift,
glad when Buddy signs off;
we can sit.

Fats Domino *Blueberry Hill* leads us into
tensing biceps and triceps with soft balls,
the colors of M &M's. We lift, breathe, bend,
count to 8 and back down, urging those
flaccid muscles to take a brief bow.

On to *Maybelline* and attempts at balance.
The boys sit and toe tap,
hands moving as if talking to the deaf.
The girls stand, grip their chairs
and tap to the code-
forward, side, back, home.
We sing along, aware the music does its work,
seducing us to move more than we want.

Jeanette Willert 63

Water bottles tip into the air...respite.
Chubby Checker gears up, invites us
to *Twist, again.* The boys sit and do their
hand jive; the girls are up and at it
shifting from foot to foot, hula hooping
their hips...though, in truth, many
agitate their lower extremities
like Maytags on slow rinse cycle.

45 minutes vanish with the music of our youth.
Cool down...*Don't it make your brown eyes blue?*
Stretch, breathe, hydrate...thank the Lord it's over.
Exit...*Earth angel, earth angel...*

Let evening come.

The idea of parallel universes

troubles me.
How would it work, I wonder,
as I weave through night curves
driving south on 231, cotton country,
rigid stubble stippling winter fields.
A half moon hangs like
a cleft marble low to the left,
its other half as much in the
unknowable dark as I.
Lights of a diner beckon in the distance,
a crossroads ahead.
Hawking would say "a peeling off point",
the possibility of an alternate me,
left or right, another path.
Likely, I will drive straight ahead, no turning,
Montgomery in the morning.

I could turn left
and go where?
Not known, not planned,
but possible.

Then?
Who would I be?
A different me?

Or to the right,
where the dark is consummate.
What path would that be?
What different self would I see?

Alternate selves, universes—
Are they always with us?

At times, temptation strikes:
to abandon a planned script and
head for Lexington or Seattle or
Toronto, spurn a flight at a layover
city.

What difference would that make?
"All the difference," Frost might have said.

Pandemic: March 26, 2020

Today, despite the tsunami of virus news,
I drive down our street of dogwoods blossoming
into our town sprayed with scarlet azaleas, weeping wisteria
and gold leaving trees. Nature is intent on being reborn
as I contemplate dying.

> *When the universe collapses, not from a meteor,*
> *but a tiny dimpled ball studded with golf tees*
> *that blossom red rosette triangles to invade our*
> *lungs paralyzing segments into stone…we are there.*

Visitors today, people I love. We sit on the porch far apart,
a bottle of sanitizer between us, a reminder of our fragile age.
A birth day for one (but we wonder, a death day hastening?).
The hunger to be together propels us to these moments of joy.

The news is dreadful. From Europe, from Asia, now US.
Not flattening, the curve (more predictive than Tiresias).
Recession spiraling into Depression tornadoes over the charts
and figures. A negligence, a punishment, a comeuppance?

> *Does the earth conspire to defeat us?*
> *Can the microbe, like the serpent,*
> *expunge us from Eden?*

Ode to the Infinite Universe

*"…we are part of the universe. We are in the universe and
the universe is in us."*

—Neil deGrasse Tyson

About loss and immortality,
Wordsworth was right:
in our day-to-day lives
we lose sight of splendor in the grass,
glory in the flower.

Yet, if we attune,
Nature will enrich us.
Viewing a young vine,
filmed at a fast speed,
tossing to and fro,
nearly dancing,
we can see
the vine seeking purchase,
spinning thin lassoes
until they stretch and catch.
Embracing a stalk or a stake
they wind ever upward
in a joyful drive,
alive!

That drive plays through us as well.
But awed by the follies of the world,
we do not sense its pulse,
the very current of spiritual being
thrumming through us, about us.

Life insists,
not just in incubators or ICU's,
but in the shoulders of bulbs
sprouting through late snow,
through migrating flocks
journeying further than great ships
just to mate, nest and bring new life,
hovering, cajoling young ones to flight.

Jeanette Willert   67

This force that flows through us all,
its energy, its certainty,
runs contrary to our notions of death.
The spark, the energy
we have thrived upon,
plays on after us,
our vessel but a temporary port.
Who are we?
A means to an end?
Are our bodies (as the leaf fallen)
fodder to be transformed
as the millennia churn on?
Our minds?
Are they the eyes of God,
messaging home?

The force that through
the green fuse flows-
flows in and through us.
Our energy moves on
though our cells. Organs perish.
This human packaging,
remains with the rock, the stream, the wind.

We are consoled
that God is in us
as we witness
the pangs of spring,
leafmeal of fall,
eternal mathematical precision
of space and matter.

www.ingramcontent.com/pod-product-compliance
Lightning Source LLC
Chambersburg PA
CBHW062152020426
42334CB00020B/2572